D1510207

SCIENCE IN THE REAL WORLD

How Do Refrigerators Work?

by **Christina Wilsdon**

Science and Curriculum Consultant: Debra Voege, M.A.,
Science Curriculum Resource Teacher

CHELSEA CLUBHOUSE

An Imprint of Chelsea House Publishers

Science in the Real World: How Do Refrigerators Work?

Chelsea Clubhouse
An imprint of Chelsea House Publishers
132 West 31st Street
New York NY 10001

Library of Congress Cataloging-in-Publication Data
Wilsdon, Christina.
    Science in the real world : how do refrigerators work? / by Christina Wilsdon;
    science and curriculum consultant, Debra Voege.
        p. cm.
    Includes index.
    ISBN 978-1-60413-473-5
  1. Refrigeration and refrigerating machinery—Juvenile literature.
  2. Refrigerators—Juvenile literature. I. Title.
  TP492.2.W55 2010
  621.5'7—dc22   2009001690

Developed for Chelsea House by RJF Publishing LLC (www.RJFpublishing.com)
Text and cover design by Tammy West/Westgraphix LLC
Illustrations by Spectrum Creative Inc.
Photo research by Edward A. Thomas
Index by Nila Glikin

Photo Credits: 4, 13, 23: © Edward A. Thomas; 5: BILL ADAMS/Newhouse News Service /Landov; 6, 10, 11: iStockphoto; 7: Library of Congress LC-USZ62-67382; 17, 25, 28: Alamy; 21: Associated Press; 24: Library of CongressLC-USZ62-71467; 26: © JVPD/0003/ImageEnvision.com; 27: Library of Congress LC-USZ62-4553; 29: Shutterstock.

Printed and bound in the United States of America

Bang RJF 10 9 8 7 6 5 4 3 2 1

This book is printed on acid-free paper.

Table of Contents

Words that are defined in the Glossary are in **bold** type
the first time they appear in the text.

Keeping Cool

What foods are in your refrigerator? Is there a carton of juice or milk? What about vegetables, fruits, meat, or cheese?

All these foods have something in common: they spoil, or "go bad," quickly if they are not kept cold. They must be chilled to keep them tasty and safe to eat. A refrigerator keeps these foods fresh by keeping them cold.

Changing the Way We Eat

Refrigerators have changed the way people eat. In the past, most fruits and vegetables could not be stored for very long. Foods such as berries, tomatoes, and lettuce were eaten only during

All kinds of foods stay fresh in a cold refrigerator.

spring and summer. In the winter, people ate a lot of foods made from grains, such as wheat and oats, because grains could be stored for a long time without spoiling.

Now, people can store many different foods for days or weeks in a refrigerator. They can store food for months in a freezer. Refrigerated fresh food can be shipped long distances in trucks and train cars. It can be sent across oceans by ships and jet planes. Ice cream trucks can bring cold treats right to your street in summer!

Thanks to refrigeration, an ice cream truck can delight people with frozen treats on a hot day.

DID YOU KNOW ?

Modern Ice Age

Refrigeration is used to chill many things besides food. Hospitals refrigerate medicines and other supplies that must be kept cold in order to work right and be safe to use. Florists refrigerate flowers to keep them fresh. Factories that make rubber for tires use refrigeration to chill batches of rubber. Air conditioners use refrigeration to cool rooms.

How Food Spoils

A freshly picked peach is sweet and tasty. But just a few days later, it starts to go bad. Soft spots form. Mold grows on it. The peach turns brown and mushy as it rots.

Rotting, or **decay**, is a natural process. Leaves that have fallen and dead plants decay outdoors. So do dead animals. Food is made from plants and animals, so it decays, too.

Some decay is caused by tiny living things called **microbes**. Microbes called **bacteria** grow in food. Other kinds of microbes make food moldy. Food spoiled by microbes may taste and smell bad. Spoiled food can also make people sick if they eat it.

Sometimes decay is caused by substances called **enzymes**. A living plant or animal makes enzymes. The enzymes keep it alive by helping it to grow or use energy. When the plant or animal is no longer

Fresh foods such as fruits spoil faster if they are not kept in a refrigerator. This spoiled orange is covered with mold.

alive and is turned into food, the enzymes cause decay instead.

Slowing Down Decay

Both microbes and enzymes are more active in warm places than in cold places. Microbes also reproduce more quickly in warm places. A food that starts out containing just a few bacteria may have

This photo from 1929 shows how Inuit in Alaska dried whale meat on a rack.

billions of bacteria after 12 hours in a warm place! But in a chilly refrigerator, decay greatly slows down.

DID YOU KNOW ?

Preserving in the Past

People living before there were refrigerators often dried foods to keep them from rotting. Drying helps preserve food because microbes like moisture. They are more active in moist food than in dry food. People dried meat and fish with sunlight, salt, or smoke from a fire. Milk was made into cheese and yogurt to make it last longer. Food was also preserved by adding certain substances, such as salt or vinegar, to it. This process is called "pickling." Microbes do not grow well in foods full of salt or vinegar, so pickled foods last longer. Plain cucumbers, for example, do not last as long as cucumbers that have been pickled to make pickles!

Refrigerators and Heat

A refrigerator is more than a box of cold air. It is actually a heat pump. A refrigerator stays chilly by soaking up heat inside it and releasing the heat into the room around it.

Normally, heat moves from a warm place to a cooler place. For example, in the winter heat from a radiator spreads out to warm up the whole room that the radiator is located in.

Refrigerant picks up heat as it flows through the freezer compartment and then releases that heat outside the refrigerator.

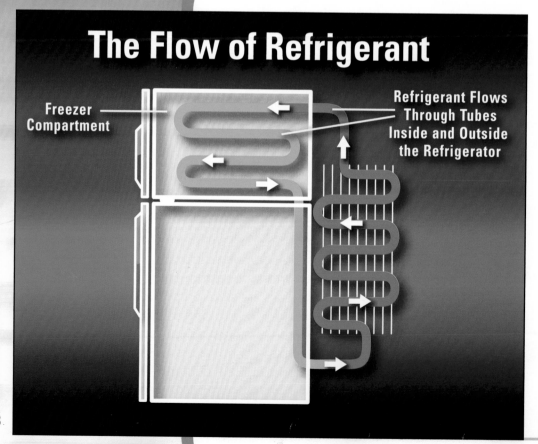

The Flow of Refrigerant

Freezer Compartment

Refrigerant Flows Through Tubes Inside and Outside the Refrigerator

But a refrigerator forces heat to move in the opposite direction. It forces heat to move from a cool place to a warmer place.

Tubes Inside and Out

The heat is carried away by a substance called **refrigerant**. Refrigerant flows through tubes in the refrigerator. Some tubes are inside the refrigerator's freezer compartment or inside its walls. Some tubes are under or behind the refrigerator, on its outside.

Refrigerant has two jobs. First it soaks up heat as it flows through the tubes inside the refrigerator. Then it lets go of this heat as it flows through the tubes on the outside.

How can one substance do both of these jobs? We will find out in the following pages how this can happen.

Mini Fridge

Heat travels from a warm place to a cooler place right inside your lunch box! This happens when you use a frozen gel pack to chill your sandwich and juice box.

The food is warmer than the gel pack. Heat travels out of the food and into the gel pack. The food gets cooler as the gel pack warms up. At lunch time, the gel pack will not be frozen anymore—but your food will feel as if it just came out of the refrigerator.

Hot and Cold

A refrigerant cools a refrigerator by changing from a liquid to a gas and back again as it travels through its tubes. It soaks up heat when it turns into a gas. Then it loses heat when it turns back into a liquid once more.

Changing from a liquid to a gas is called **evaporation**. Your body uses evaporation to cool you off on a hot day. On a hot day, sweat trickles out of your skin. Then it turns into a gas called water vapor. This change uses heat energy. The heat comes from your skin. The vapor carries away

Wet sheets and other items that are hung on a clothesline will dry because the sun's heat makes the water in them evaporate.

heat as it drifts into the air. This makes you feel a little bit cooler.

Just the Opposite

The opposite happens when a gas turns into a liquid. Changing from a gas to a liquid is called **condensation**. You can see condensation on the side of a cold glass on a hot day. Water vapor in the air turns into a liquid when it touches the cold glass. It condenses into water droplets. This change gives off heat. The heat moves into the glass. It makes the cool drink in the glass get warmer, too.

Water vapor condenses on the side of a cold glass. It changes from an invisible gas to liquid drops of water.

DID YOU KNOW ?

Boiling Cold!

What happens to water that is heated in a kettle? It gets hotter and hotter until it finally turns into a gas. This gas comes out of the spout and makes the kettle whistle! This happens when the water reaches a temperature of 212°F (100°C). We say that the water is boiling.

We think of "boiling" as hot because water boils at such a high temperature. But other liquids boil at much lower temperatures. In fact, a refrigerant boils at a temperature far below the freezing point of water, which is 32°F (0°C). That's why a liquid refrigerant can boil, or turn into a gas, even inside a chilly refrigerator.

Under Pressure

Heating a liquid can change it into a gas. Cooling a gas can change it into a liquid. But a refrigerator does not cook refrigerant to turn it into a gas. It does not chill refrigerant to turn it into a liquid. Instead, a refrigerator uses **pressure** to change the refrigerant.

Pressure is the amount of force pressing on something. When you blow up a balloon, you are using air pressure to fill it. The balloon inflates a little at first. The pressure in the balloon grows as you blow in more air. Slowly, the balloon gets larger and firmer. If you keep blowing, the pressure grows until the balloon pops.

Changing Pressure

Air pressure affects liquids and gases, too. Lowering pressure can make a liquid evaporate. Increasing pressure can make a gas turn into a liquid.

A refrigerator turns refrigerant into a gas and then back into a liquid by changing the pressure. It makes

The pressure of air pushing on a balloon's stretchy skin makes the balloon get larger. A refrigerator uses air pressure to make its refrigerant change from gas to liquid and back again.

the refrigerant switch between soaking up heat and letting it go. The pressure changes happen in different parts of the refrigerator.

DID YOU KNOW ?

Cooking in the Mountains

Even though you can't see it, air presses on you and everything around you. The weight of air pressure depends on where you are. Air pressure is lower on a mountaintop than on a beach. The difference in pressure affects how water boils. There is less pressure on water in a cooking pot on a mountain. Less pressure means the water can boil at a lower temperature. Water normally boils at 212°F (100°C), but water may boil at just 187°F (86°C) on a high mountaintop.

The Evaporator: Low Pressure

The **evaporator** is a wide tube that loops through the walls of a refrigerator's freezer section. Its name is a clue to its job: refrigerant evaporates inside it. It needs energy, in the form of heat, to evaporate.

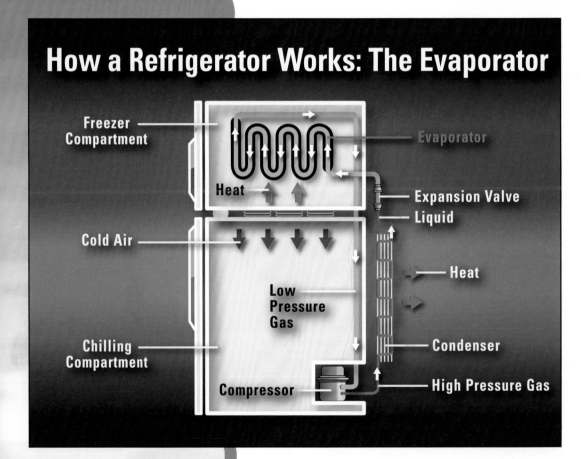

How a Refrigerator Works: The Evaporator

Freezer Compartment

Evaporator

Heat

Expansion Valve

Liquid

Cold Air

Heat

Low Pressure Gas

Chilling Compartment

Condenser

Compressor

High Pressure Gas

In the evaporator, outlined in black in this picture, refrigerant flowing through tubes in the freezer compartment absorbs heat as it turns into a gas. This gas then flows down a tube inside the refrigerator's back wall to a device called the compressor.

The refrigerant gets this heat from food and air in the freezer. It absorbs the heat, which makes the freezer get colder. The evaporator's tubes get colder, too. As they get colder, even more heat leaves the freezer, because heat travels from warmer places to colder places.

From a Liquid to a Gas

The refrigerant doesn't store all this heat. It uses most of the heat to change from a liquid to a gas as it travels through the evaporator.

Next, the refrigerant travels down a tube in the wall of the refrigerator's lower section. It is still a cool gas under low pressure. This tube takes it to the **compressor**.

Cold, But Not Frozen

A refrigerator's freezer is colder than its chilling section. Cold air made in the freezer cools the chilling section under it because cold air sinks. The sinking air flows through special gaps, or vents, between the two sections. This air moving from the freezer makes the chilling section cold enough (below 40°F, or 4°C) to keep food fresh. A fan also helps blow the cold air. This helps the cold air spread evenly through the refrigerator. Refrigerators with freezers on the bottom or on the side also use fans to move cold air into the chilling section and all around it.

The Compressor: High Pressure

In the evaporator, the refrigerant evaporated. In the compressor, it's compressed! The compressor is a pump that is run by an electric motor. "Compress" means to squash or squeeze. A compressor squeezes refrigerant by forcing it into a smaller space.

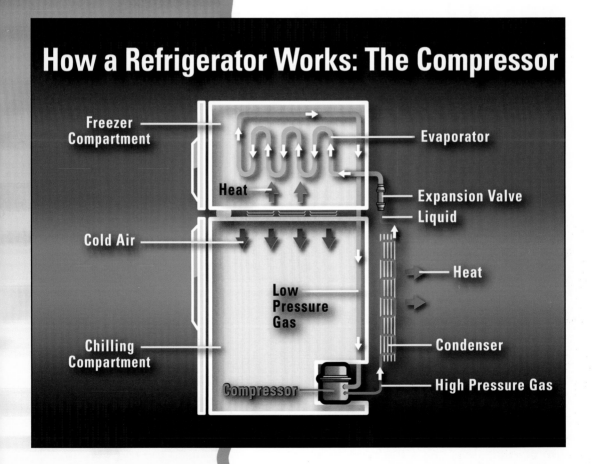

How a Refrigerator Works: The Compressor

- Freezer Compartment
- Evaporator
- Heat
- Expansion Valve
- Liquid
- Cold Air
- Heat
- Low Pressure Gas
- Chilling Compartment
- Condenser
- Compressor
- High Pressure Gas

In the compressor, outlined in black in this picture, the refrigerant is squeezed, or compressed. It becomes a high-pressure gas, and it becomes warmer.

The compressor pulls refrigerant out of the evaporator when it runs. The refrigerant is still a cool, low-pressure gas at this point. The pressure is low because the gas had lots of room in the evaporator.

The compressor is the black machine at the bottom of this refrigerator.

High Pressure

But now the compressor squeezes it into a smaller space. This puts the refrigerant under high pressure. High pressure doesn't just squeeze the refrigerant. It also raises its temperature. The refrigerant is still a gas, but now it is a hot gas instead of a cool one.

You can hear the compressor when it runs. It makes a humming noise.

DID YOU KNOW ?

Compressing Air

You can feel how air heats up when it is under high pressure by pumping up a bicycle tire with a bicycle pump. The pump squeezes air into a smaller space. The air is under high pressure as it goes from the pump into the tire. Touch the connection between the pump and the tire. You will feel that some parts are warm. This is heat caused by compressing the air.

The Condenser: *More* High Pressure

The **condenser** is a thin tube that loops back and forth. It is attached to the outside of the refrigerator, either on the back or underneath.

Just like the evaporator and the compressor, the condenser has a name that is a clue to its job. It is where refrigerant condenses. The refrigerant goes from being a gas to being a liquid again.

When the refrigerant left the compressor, it was a hot gas under high pressure. It is still a high-pressure, hot gas when it flows into the condenser. The hot refrigerant heats up the condenser as it flows through it.

Losing Heat

But now the refrigerant begins to lose its heat, because heat travels from warmer places to cooler places. The refrigerant is hotter than the air in the room, so heat leaves the condenser. You can feel this heat coming out of the back or bottom of a refrigerator.

How a Refrigerator Works: The Condenser

Freezer Compartment

Evaporator

Heat

Expansion Valve

Liquid

Cold Air

Heat

Low Pressure Gas

Chilling Compartment

Condenser

Compressor

High Pressure Gas

As it loses its heat, the refrigerant condenses. It turns back into a liquid. So the refrigerant is a liquid again by the time it reaches the end of the condenser and is ready to go back into the refrigerator.

As the refrigerant flows through the condenser, outlined in black, it loses heat and goes from being a gas to being a liquid.

DID YOU KNOW ?

Refrigerants Then and Now

Early refrigerators used dangerous chemicals as refrigerants. They were harmful to breathe and burned easily. They worked fine inside a refrigerator but were dangerous if they leaked out. In the 1930s, new refrigerants called chlorofluorocarbons replaced them. They are known as CFCs for short. CFCs were later found to harm a part of Earth's atmosphere called the ozone layer. This layer shields Earth from some of the Sun's harmful rays. Today, refrigerators use different refrigerants and not CFCs. The newest refrigerants do not harm the ozone layer.

Back to the Evaporator

T he refrigerant is a cool liquid when it comes to the end of the condenser. But it is still under high pressure. The refrigerant needs to evaporate so that it can keep cooling the refrigerator.

The cool, liquid refrigerant flows back into the evaporator through a very skinny tube called an **expansion valve**. This small tube is thinner than the condenser tube. It is much thinner than the evaporator tube. It is just large enough for the refrigerant to squeeze through.

At the end of the condenser, the refrigerant goes through a very thin tube called the expansion valve, outlined in black in this picture. It shoots out of the expansion valve and into the evaporator as tiny drops of liquid. Under low pressure again, it turns into a gas and takes heat from the freezer.

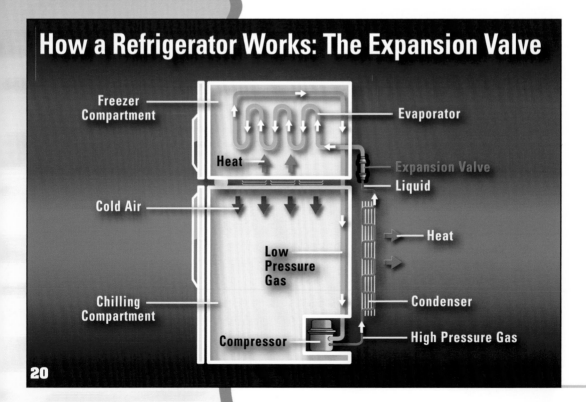

How a Refrigerator Works: The Expansion Valve

- Freezer Compartment
- Evaporator
- Heat
- Expansion Valve
- Liquid
- Cold Air
- Heat
- Low Pressure Gas
- Condenser
- Chilling Compartment
- Compressor
- High Pressure Gas

The refrigerant moves through this tiny tube quickly because it is under high pressure. It shoots out the other side, into the evaporator. It sprays out as tiny drops of liquid, like mist from a can of air freshener.

This baby mammoth lay frozen in the snow and ice of the Arctic ever since it died 10,000 years ago. Because the body was frozen, it did not rot away, and scientists can study it to learn about the past.

Cooling the Freezer Again

When the liquid refrigerant bursts out of the skinny tube and into the wide pipe of the evaporator, it is suddenly in a low-pressure area again. Without a lot of pressure squeezing it, the refrigerant quickly starts turning into a gas.

Meanwhile, the refrigerant starts using heat energy as it evaporates. It starts pulling heat out of the freezer. The refrigeration cycle continues.

DID YOU KNOW ?

Brrr!

Food can be stored for months in a freezer without spoiling. In the wild, ice and snow work like freezers, too. In the cold northern lands of the Arctic, scientists have dug up the frozen bodies of woolly mammoths. Mammoths are animals like elephants that became **extinct**, or completely died out, thousands of years ago. The animals found by scientists have been dead for thousands of years, but the cold preserved their skin, fur, and other body parts.

Temperature Control

A refrigerator has to keep track of its temperature so that its freezer and chilling section are always cold. This job is done by a part that is called a **thermostat**. It measures the temperature inside the refrigerator, just as a thermostat in a room measures the room's temperature.

Most refrigerators have just one thermostat. It measures the temperature in the freezer section. The coldness of the freezer is used to cool the chilling section, too. So if the freezer is very cold, then the chilling section will be just right. Some new refrigerators, however, have thermostats in both sections.

If the refrigerator is cold enough, the thermostat turns off the compressor. If the refrigerator is getting too warm, the thermostat turns on the compressor.

A thermostat in a room works in much the same way. In winter, it turns a furnace on and off. In summer, in houses that have air conditioning, a thermostat turns the air conditioner on and off.

Warm Air Slips in

After the refrigerant has made the inside of the refrigerator cold, why would the refrigerator get warmer again? A refrigerator's temperature will slowly go up over time because heat flows into it from the room around it. Warmer air flows in every time the refrigerator door is opened. A little warm air also slips in around the door even when the door is shut.

This happens even though a refrigerator door is designed to keep out as much warm air as possible when the door is closed. Its edges are lined with a rubbery strip called a **gasket**. The gasket seals the door when it is shut. The door's edges also contain magnets. The magnets give the door extra grip to shut tightly.

A dollar bill is gripped tightly by a closed refrigerator door with a good seal. If the dollar slides out easily, that is a sign that the door is leaky and needs a new gasket.

DID YOU KNOW ?

Checking the Gasket

Gaskets can wear out and allow more warm air from the room to get inside the refrigerator. You can do a simple test to see how good your refrigerator's seal is. Shut the door on a dollar bill. If you can pull the dollar out easily, the gasket may be "leaky" and need to be replaced.

Refrigeration in the Past

People have chilled food since ancient times to keep it from spoiling.

About 3,000 years ago, people in China cooled food with ice. They cut the ice from frozen lakes. Then they packed it into cool, dark pits to keep it from melting quickly. Wealthy people in ancient Greece and Rome sipped cool drinks in summertime thanks to snow and ice brought down from mountaintops. People living in cold northern lands let meat freeze in the ice and snow around them.

This ice house dates back to the 1700s. It was used to store ice cut from a pond for the use of a wealthy family in France.

Ice Houses

Ice was stored in ice houses in parts of Europe. An ice house was like a big picnic cooler. Inside, ice cut from frozen lakes and rivers in winter was covered with

sawdust, cloth, or other materials that slowed the flow of heat into the ice. Materials that slow heat flow are called **insulation**.

People in parts of America also cut and stored ice in the 1700s and 1800s. Ice was cut from ponds and lakes in northern areas with cold winters. Some was packed and shipped by train to cities and to warm southern areas. In the late 1800s, ice was even cut and shipped across the ocean to Europe!

Before there were refrigerators, people got ice from frozen lakes in the winter. These people are cutting blocks of ice from a lake in Pennsylvania in 1907.

DID YOU KNOW ?

The First "Refrigerator"

In 1803, a Maryland farmer named Thomas Moore invented a device that he called a refrigerator. It was a wooden tub filled with ice. Moore put butter from his farm into the tub. Then he put the tub in a metal box and covered it with rabbit fur. The refrigerator kept the butter cold on long trips to town on market days. People eagerly bought Moore's cold, fresh butter instead of the soft, melted butter offered by other farmers.

Iceboxes

The first refrigerators appeared in American kitchens in the 1830s. They were called iceboxes—and that's just what they were: boxes with chunks of ice inside.

An icebox was usually made of wood. The box was lined with metal or another waterproof material. Cork, straw, or other insulation filled the space between the wall and the lining.

In old-fashioned ice boxes like this one, a big block of ice would sit on the top shelf. As it melted, the ice chilled the air around it, which kept food in the ice box cold.

A Better Icebox

The first iceboxes simply held a block of ice that chilled food near it. Later, iceboxes were built with a shelf at the top for the ice.

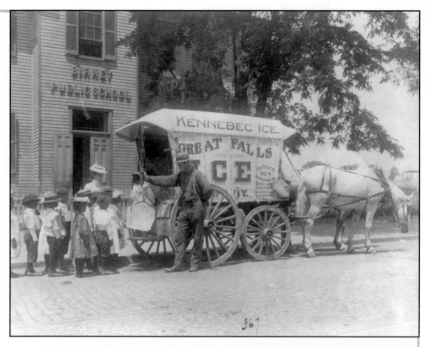

The ice cooled air near it. The cold air dropped down to the bottom of the icebox, where food was stored.

The cold air pushed warmer air out of its way when it sank. It forced the warmer air to rise and be cooled by the ice at top. In this way, the air went around inside the icebox, keeping food cool as the ice melted.

An iceman used a horse and wagon to deliver ice to businesses and homes for their ice boxes. This iceman is using tongs to hold a block of ice and show it to a group of schoolchildren in 1899.

DID YOU KNOW ?

The Iceman

Ice for iceboxes was delivered by an iceman. He carried the ice in a wagon pulled by a horse. In summer, kids often followed the wagon, hoping to get a chip of ice as a treat.

The iceman lifted a block of ice by gripping it with a pair of **tongs**. Then he carried it on his back into the home. The block of ice lasted two or three days. A pan under the icebox caught the water that dripped from the melting ice.

Electric Refrigerators

In 1834, inventor Jacob Perkins built a machine that cooled air inside it. The machine had a compressor attached to a **crank**. It worked when the crank was turned. Liquid in the machine evaporated and cooled the air.

But it wasn't until the early 1900s that refrigerators with compressors were used in home kitchens. By 1916, these refrigerators were powered by electricity. At first, only rich people had these refrigerators. But by the 1930s, refrigerators cost less. The most popular one was a refrigerator with a compressor perched on its top. It was called the Monitor Top.

In this picture from the 1930s, a salesman shows a customer the features of the newest refrigerator of that time.

Bigger and Better

Since that time, refrigerators have changed a lot. Today's refrigerators are bigger than earlier ones and can hold more food. Special features have been added, such as ice makers. Modern refrigerators also use less energy than refrigerators did just 20 years ago.

Today, about 132 million refrigerators are found in homes across the United States. Refrigerators are also at work in restaurants and in stores of all kinds that sell food. Can you imagine the ways our lives would change without them?

Today's refrigerators are bigger and better than earlier models.

DID YOU KNOW ?

Tiny Refrigerators in Space

Scientists have built very small refrigerators called "cryocoolers" for use in space. They are not for cooling food. They are used to cool scientific tools that heat up as they work. Some of these tools are parts of **telescopes** and cameras. They do not work properly if they are too warm. One cryocooler is no more than 5 inches (12.5 centimeters) long. It can reach a low temperature of -370°F (-223°C). That is about as cold as icy Pluto far out in space.

Glossary

bacteria—Tiny, one-celled living things that can be seen only with a microscope and are often called "germs."

compressor—The part of a refrigerator that turns **refrigerant** into a hot, high-pressure gas.

condensation—The changing of a gas to a liquid.

condenser—The part of a refrigerator where **refrigerant** goes from being a gas to being a liquid, losing heat in the process.

crank—A handle that can be turned to make something move or work, such as a machine or a part of a machine.

decay—The rotting, or breaking down, of a substance.

enzymes—Substances found in living things that help chemical reactions happen.

evaporation—The changing of a liquid to a gas.

evaporator—The part of a refrigerator where **refrigerant** goes from being a liquid to being a gas, absorbing heat in the process.

expansion valve—The thin tube that **refrigerant** goes through to get back into the evaporator.

extinct—Completely died out; a kind of animal or plant that no longer exists is said to have become extinct.

gasket—Something made of rubber, metal, or another material that seals the edges of a container to keep heat or a gas or a liquid from getting in or out; a gasket on a refrigerator door keeps warm air out and cold air in.

insulation—Materials that help slow down the flow of heat from one place to another.

microbes—Tiny living things that can be seen individually only with a microscope.

pressure—A force that presses on substances.

refrigerant—A liquid that turns into a gas at a low temperature and can be used for chilling the air inside a refrigerator.

refrigeration—The cooling of an area and anything inside that area.

telescope—A device for looking at objects that are very far away.

thermostat—A device that senses temperature changes and turns another device on or off to control the temperature.

tongs—A tool with two arms that is used to grab or lift something.